Neck Top Programming

The Secret to a Winning Mindset

Don't Try & Lose

PAULINE GINNELLY

Illustration by Kyle C Macpherson

- At half time -

About the Author

Pauline Ginnelly is a Self Development Coach.
Her clients range from children & families to individuals
& even pets.

With over 10 years experience helping people create Change,
She is available for one to one sessions and also runs
her own unique Success4Self Group workshops.

Living with her 4 legged friends
Joules the Bichon and Wookiee the Lhasa

After initially training in Hypnotherapy & NLP
with Tom McKay of McKay Solutions
and Gary Craig for EFT – Emotional Freedom Technique
Pauline was fortunate to be invited to train
with renowned Trainer & Author Terence Watts
on his revolutionary Coaching Technique –   SymbioDynamics
and as a result is proud to be

Scotland 1st SymbioDynamics Practitioner.

Copyright © 2012 Pauline Ginnelly

Success4Self

All rights reserved

ISBN:13: 9781481012508

ISBN:10: 1481012509

ACKNOWLEDGEMENTS

With love and thanks to my my son Kyle
who has always been my number one fan
-I love you dearly -
& You'll always be my greatest achievement
I hope you are now as proud of me as I am you.
The support & encouragement you gave me
from the very beginning
& the many hours spent bouncing my ideas around
was what gave me the self belief
to share my thoughts & theories in this book.

To my fantastic family/friends
who put up with my eccentric ways
– even those friends I no longer see -
Thank you all for your help & support over the years

To my clients
Past, Present & Future,
I am grateful for the opportunity to work with you
& Thank you for your co-operation & feedback

To the Universe
Thank you for delivering my requests

For more information or to book Pauline go to
www.Success4Self.co.uk

or find her on facebook.

CONTENTS

	Acknowledgments	Pg 5
	Foreword	Pg 9
1	Mans Machine	Pg 13
2	3 Layers – Operating System	Pg 19
3	Processor, RAM	Pg 23
4	Operator	Pg 33
5	Hands Free	Pg 47
6	Intention	Pg 49
7	Words	Pg 59
8	Programming Others	Pg 113
9	The Key	Pg 117
10	The Magic number 3	Pg 125
11	Symbolism	Pg 131

FOREWORD

This book is the information Pauline shares with every client
before a session

Because her research has indicated it is crucial to enable success
in all areas of life

Here you have the opportunity to discover
how it is you may have been accidentally programming yourself
and others to make success more difficult

Within this short book is enough information to enable you
to begin to create the changes in your responses and behaviours
in life you desire

Simple Explanations and Practical Instructions
on how you can make very small changes internally

And experience DRAMATIC changes to your daily life

When people discover this - they often think
it's too easy to be true

But the proof is in the pudding so to speak.

We accept we have to periodically clear out our cupboards,

We accept we periodically clear out our attics and garages

We know we have to Clear out programs, files, cookies
& internet history from our PC every now and then

Yet how many of us ever have took the time to

clear out our minds?

You're probably aware you have 'stuff' within your mind
that affects your success today

'Stuff' leftover from the past
that is possibly no longer valid   or productive

Yet we have no instructions or knowledge
on how to clear this rubbish out

So we can update our mind -
with new improved PRODUCTIVE programs

Programs that enable us to feel good on a daily basis

Programs **that propel us to Success Easily & Naturally**

In this I am going to give my theory on the human mind,
and how it can be likened to a computer.

Way more than perhaps you may already realise.

And I'll explain how, more often than not
we go through our daily life without realising
how **we're affecting** the 'running' of this *neck top computer*...

How quite often we're 'programming' ourselves for failure -
or at least 'programming' ourselves
to make it *more difficult to succeed*

Accidentally of course

We're doing this *accidental programming* to ourselves,

to our friends - and to our children.

From the moment we begin communicating with them!

Read my theory on this and

Don't just take my word for it

GO OUT AND TEST IT.

Test it

And you'll be amazed for yourself to discover how
this really does seem to have an effect on your outcome..

1

MANS MACHINE

Your brain can be likened
to the most powerful computer system ever created

If you think about it - even the very best computer created,
has originated from within *the creators imagination.*

Someone has to *imagine everything in* their minds eye,
before it can ever exist in the real world.

Every single man made object has came from the imagination
of a human mind.

Things like tables, tv's, clothes, cars, planes, wind turbines,

whoopee cushions, electric fences, shoes,

central heating........ the list is endless.

Every single legend, fairy tale or myth passed down
from Generation to Generation
has **came from** the creative *imagination of a human mind.*

Every piece of music **started its life**
within the imagination of the human mind.

Every delicious or disgusting food recipe ever tried or tested
was **first created** *within the imagination.*

These of course are only the things we have *right now*
at this time in our evolution.

There are many more brand new 'dreams'
or concepts being created,
every single moment within human minds everywhere
around the planet.

Everything that exists around us
has been created, developed
or adapted by the human imagination.

Or is about to be..

Back to computers

Most people are familiar with 'Desktop' or 'Laptop' computers.

But I want to draw your attention to **your very own computer**

THE MOST POWERFUL PC THERE IS.

The personal computer *you were born with*

The personal computer that is *always switched on & running*

The personal computer you *take everywhere* with you.

The computer you use *all day everyday*
without a second thought.

YOUR NECK TOP COMPUTER

We use it to process everything
from outside and inside ourselves,
hundreds of times a minute - For our entire lives.

Mostly without our conscious awareness.

Your 'neck top' computer *(your mind)*
is more like a computer than perhaps you've given it credit for

A powerful fast reliable machine

But like all machines
It relies on competent operators
If someone with no previous experience
or idea about computers sat down in front of a PC
and started accidentally putting in commands
that made no sense to the PC -

Nothing would happen - *At best*

At worst -
the pc would respond to the commands it did recognise
and that could, in turn cause some malfunction

And like any other machine that needs an operator
Our neck top will respond to everything we put in
CORRECTLY

Its programmed to never stop responding
Running thoughts, ideas and reactions
to what's happening outside ourselves

As well as responding to what we are saying to ourselves
on the inside
and what's going on in there!

THAT'S WHY
IT IS CRUCIAL WE HAVE SOME IDEA
OF HOW WE ARE
PROGRAMMING OUR FUTURE GENERATIONS

Instead of sending them out into the world
Expecting them to Achieve Success somehow
with little or no instructions or clue
on *how to run their neck top computer*
to get the best out of it
so they can find school work easier perhaps,
or be better at sports.

We would never dream of letting our children loose
on our expensive laptop or desktop computers.
Least not until they know how to use it properly
until they are **Competent Operators**
otherwise we are at risk of them doing some damage

Yet this fundamentally is what we are doing to our children,
we are sending them off to school to have success
UNKNOWINGLY *in charge* of a powerful tool
that when used correctly
will deliver success easily and naturally

2

THREE MAIN LAYERS

Just like any desktop or laptop computer

There are layers to your neck top to enable it to function as we know it

LAYER ONE -

OPERATING SYSTEM = THE UNCONSCIOUS MIND

Starting at the very 'back' - The *unseen* part of your laptop and its 'make up'

There is the 'Operating System'

WIN 98/ XP/ VISTA

Or apple, Linux etc

We cannot 'see' this operating system -
It 'runs' automatically in the background

We don't have to do anything to it (if set on automatic updates)

We simply expect it to be 'there' when we need it -
Doing whatever it is that it does.

But we're aware that we *need it in order to use the computer*
We could do nothing
if this operating system were not fully operating

This *'Operating System'* is the equivalent on your 'neck top'
to your UNCONSCIOUS MIND

This is the part of your mind that

BEATS YOUR HEART, PUMPS YOUR BLOOD,
GROWS YOUR HAIR, HEALS YOUR SKIN,
BREAKS DOWN YOUR FOOD,
CONTROLS THE TEMPRATURE OF YOUR BODY,
MAINTAINS THE HORMONE LEVELS OF YOUR BODY
etc

We can 'see' none of this happening - We do little to control it
It all *runs automatically in the background*
You cannot speed up your pulse just by *willing* it to happen…..

Try it for yourself now
speed up your pulse as your sitting here reading this…..

Any change??

This is not something you are In *conscious control* of

But I'm sure you will agree
that if it were not for this 'operating system'
we call our unconscious mind

Doing whatever it is it does *in the background* -

We would not be able to *function* on a daily basis

Things we take for granted
Like breathing, walking, speaking and eating
would require such incredible effort and concentration from us.

Therefore preventing us from being able to just spontaneously do the these things

WHILST still doing other things too…..

Think about it …..

If we had to take conscious control of the very basic tasks of breathing for instance,
would take so much concentration and attention

We would struggle to *even think about doing anything else*

Whereas we take *our operating system* for granted

We multi task constantly throughout the day -

Trusting our unconscious mind will take care of those automatic processes in our bodies

Probably never even giving them a second thought

More often than not these unconscious automatic processes are never considered

Until a problem or issues arises with them

Then suddenly we become aware of just how often we require them

It's not until a part of out mind or body
*is n*ot functioning as it was/should

That we pay any attention to it -

and realise how well it can   or did work!

3

MEGABYTES/RAM/PROCESSOR = SUBCONSIOUS MIND

LAYER TWO

Within our desktops and laptops
There's much importance put on the processor speed
and the size of the memory (megabytes of RAM)

This put simply -
is how much 'stuff' you can store or file away
and how fast you can access it all.

However advancements in the capabilities of the *Processor*
is crucial also

For a huge memory is one thing

But if you have a very *slow processor* ……

Then you'll perhaps
only actually be able to 'run' one or two programs at a time

If this is true for your computer at work or at home -
then you'll know how slow and frustrating that can be!!!!

*Although I am no computer expert -
I do know that they work with numbers and letters
they need 'sets' of these in a particular sequence
to enable a program to 'run'

Our 'neck top' equivalent to the processor and the megabytes
is our *SUBCONSCIOUS MIND*

The **subconscious** is the part of us
responsible for *what* we remember
And *how* we remember it

However instead of using letters and numbers

The subconscious mind learns and remembers
through our 5 senses.

Storing good and bad feelings, images, sounds and smells
in the memory.

Often these images are *symbolic*
and *not an image of the actual memory.*

Almost like a ZIP file on a computer -

Where a HUGE amount of information can be compressed down into a small 'holding' file called a ZIP therefore taking up less space on the memory

Of course we have to UNZIP these files to view or use.

Our memories are like the ZIP files of our life -

Often they contain HUGE amounts of information regarding our thoughts, feelings, facts, figures etc.

this explains how an item of clothing can remind you of a holiday, or a particular music track can evoke memories of a whole relationship

Feelings and images are a lot easier for us to use than the numbers and letters

Because we make up our own sequences within our neck top

We are effectively programming ourselves for the tomorrow.

By 'storing' specific images sounds and feelings
that will evoke a specific memory or feeling in the future

Or 'run' a particular response within us -
such as fear of something like spiders.

Even *a whole lifetime* of these internal representations
made up of images, sounds, smells and feelings
GOOD AND BAD...

Only take up a percentage of the 'physical space' taken up
by the average human head

Which is smaller than the average PC tower!!

So our subconscious mind is like our processor and our
memory store

And mostly -if used properly (like all computers)
This works very well

We can 'process' and remember many things at the same time

We can for example -

TIE OUR SHOELACES
FEEL THE TEMPRATURE IN THE ROOM
DECIDE WHAT WE WANT FOR BREAKFAST
(COMPARE THAT TO YESTERDAYS & TOMMORROWS)
REMIND OURSELVES WE HAVE TO PUT BIN OUT
TASTE THE MOUTHWASH WE JUST USED
HUMM OR WHISTLE TO OURSELVES
FEEL HUNGRY
HAVE AN UNDERLYING SENSE OF SADNESS/ANGER
FEEL PAIN

ALL THIS
WHILST ACCESSING 'HOW' WE FEEL RIGHT NOW…..

Of course we are **still** automatically

beating our heart,

pumping our blood,

growing our hair

and fighting off that cold

Think of how many dual layer processors needed
in the average computer
to be doing the equivalent amount of tasks at the same time

SURFING THE NET
DOWNLOADING A MOVIE
LISTENING TO MUSIC
COMPOSING AN EMAIL
TRANSFERING PHOTOS
BURNING A CD
UPDATING SOFTWARE
RECEIVING EMAIL
CHATTING ONLINE
DELETING A PROGRAM
INSTALLING A PROGRAM
UPDATING A PROGRAM

ALL SIMULTANIOUSLY

The only PC capable of doing ALL that
And more at the same time

Is our own neck top version --

Constantly designers are working to improve
the laptop and desktops capability for multi tasking.

Because constantly
we want faster response from the machines we buy.

No sooner than you get your new PC home from the shop
and set it up.

It is almost out of date!

Often the very software you have to load onto it -
is advertising the new updated version
of the very thing your putting on !!!

Unlike our own neck top model,
Constantly upgradable and expandable

We can learn new skills and abilities At any time during our life

We can train our brains = scientist have proven that.

Although mostly we seem to live our lives
as if we have no control over our minds

No control over our reactions

Maybe even no control over our results

However this is most definitely UNTRUE

Many of us never stop to think that
when we react to things in life....
when we feel ourselves become angry or offended, upset or sad

We are not reacting to what's happening to or around us,

but infact

We react to what we say to ourselves about it'

Think about this scenario -

Your sitting with someone say your friend or your therapist
And they get up out of the blue and come across the room
and SLAP your face

NOW

There will be a pause
while you consider what just happened to you
You'll have a decision to make *after* this consideration

So you TALK it over with yourself

You may say something like " funny therapy this"
- and decide to laugh

Or

" WTF how dare you" and decide to get up and retaliate

Or

" OMG! I cant believe that just happened" and you leave

But think about it - In order to decide
if your going to find it funny, insulting or aggressive…

You will have to TALK TO YOURSELF ABOUT IT FIRST!

So therefore

We are not reacting to what goes on around us in the world,
or what happens to us in it…

But infact
We're reacting to what we SAY TO OURSELVES ABOUT IT!

4

LAYER THREE

OPERATOR = CONSCIOUS MIND

The most obvious essential 'layer'
of our everyday computers 'make up' is the Operator

The person who sits down in front of the computer
And inputs to the machine what's required

- Through the use of a mouse and keyboard mainly -
Although there are developments in the computer 'world'
to eliminate the need for a keyboard/mouse
& only a blink of the eye will do the equivalent

The letters and numbers sequences we put into our pc
Instructs the computer what to use or open or 'run'

Just like the little icon we click on our pc screen
starts a particular program or application

Various menus, tools and applications can be accessed
simply through a click of a mouse button

Each click or 'run' command that is applied by the operator -
Is unquestioned by the computer

No matter how advanced the computer is
They are simply not capable of reasoning with us

Or refusing to do a particular action

For example

A computer will allow *any operator* access to any of its files,
folders and applications -

Provided the Operator has correctly entered the security
requirements

Of course these security measures - no matter how strong
Are still *man made* none the less.

Or at least the very programs that control them
And would not be present at all
If previously someone hadn't put the security measures in place.

Just the same if a child (or an adult)
were to pass these security measures

Then instruct the PC to do something *illegal* or *immoral*

Such as download copyright music or material
Watch or download pornographic material
Send or receive illegal material

The computer **will follow** those illegal or immoral instructions.

Similarly the computer will not 'refuse' to do something
if it has previously been programmed to do so

Unless there is a problem or a virus that prevents it

And if you ask a computer to do one thing after another -

Even if its Very quickly
(you may have done this in a situation where you've been
impatient waiting on 'stuff' opening and you question if the PC
has even registered your 'click')

BUT

Every individual click you made

Every 'run' you set into action

Will open or run..

As soon as the computer can do it

As soon as there's a little space

UP IT WILL POP

The application or program you clicked AGES ago!

Even if you'd changed your mind since you clicked it
And you no longer require it

You are unable to stop it

You clicked it -so it will open or run -

And **only then** can you close or stop it..

Think about this ……..

If a computer *was* capable of reasoning with us

Then the illegal activities that are rife within computers, and the internet

Would NOT happen

Simple - **the computer would 'refuse'**

Of course the only way this could probably happen,
is if the computer could be built
with the security for this capability already in place

Really then of course all that would happen

Is the computer would simply be built without a cd or dvd rom, email access, internet access or a large memory to store files

BUT WHO WOULD WANT SUCH A COMPUTER??

We all want access and the capability to email and surf,
to save and store.

So if the computer *is built with the ability to do this initially*.

It's then UNABLE to refuse a 'command'
to execute a particular task within its capability.

This is exactly the same within our own neck top PC

Unfortunately it's incapable of reasoning with us either

Whenever we're reasoning or analyzing a situation

We're using our conscious mind only

Our subconscious and our unconscious
Are both unable to reason or debate with us.

No matter how 'in tune' we are with ourselves

Again,

If our neck top *was* capable of reasoning with us
it would be capable of preventing us
from doing something destructive to ourselves
Something such as smoking, alcoholism
Or injecting drugs into our bodies...
would somehow be intervened by our neck top automatically

Or even using the laptop or desktop PC
to download illegal images or material

We would be unable to open our eyes -
No matter how much we tried

We would be unable to see

and our neck top would be responsible for causing this reaction

If this were to happen -

Every time we were to look at something illegal for example

We would soon stop wasting our time looking

But of course this is ridiculous

Because we are in charge of our eyes

And although blinking is automatic,

as a general rule whenever we wanted to -

We can open and close them

We decide this

Or for example if

every time a heroin addict went to 'jack up'

Their neck top PC immediately creates a spasm
within that specific area

And made it **repeatedly impossible** for them to do it

This would likely prevent a lot of people becoming addicts

But again this does not happen

We are in control of our bodies
and what we put into them

Even if we know that its bad for our health or even killing us.

That's why we can smoke

over eat, under exercise, take drugs,

Even to the extent of crimes

If our neck top pc **was** capable of refusing
and effectively **preventing us** doing illegal or immoral activities

That would inevitably lead
to a disappearance of crime completely

Because no one would commit them

Their neck top simply wouldn't allow them

There would be **no need for police,**

or any other form of order/control or indeed punishment

Of course this is *not reality*

People do commit crimes
People do smoke knowing it causes cancer
People take drugs knowing they're illegal and dangerous
People do download and share illegal/immoral images/material
People do overeat knowing it'll make them miserable tomorrow

If only our neck top could stop us doing these behaviors

After all most of us don't want to do them

We feel trapped or addicted
Almost like we cannot stop even though we really want to..

When infact perhaps
it could simply be a matter of the programs your running

Some of them

like smoking for example
Are literally *'pinned to your start menu'*

So you do this behaviour automatically

With very little thought from you

Just as it is for brushing your teeth
or Eating with a knife and fork

All these 'programs' we had learn and install
at some point previously

Through repetition - Over and over -
Until it became a habit

And then once the habit is formed -

It requires no more effort or thought from you

Its almost like that installed program
is now permanently pinned to your start menu

Imagine this scenario for a moment........

You work with computers
And everyday for many years without problem,
You start your day by typing in - www.Google.com

But one day for whatever reason
Your not paying attention to what your typing

And by accident you write - www.Giggle.com

Now you probably will already know

The computer will not reason or debate this with you

No matter
that you have NEVER used Giggle.com previously

And it is ALWAYS www.Google.com you start with

WHY WOULD YOU WANT GIGGLE.COM??

This is irrelevant to the computer

Because it does not have the ability to KNOW
that Giggle is NOT what you want

Now because its built to follow commands if given,
then all that computer is capable of giving you
Is the results it has for www.Giggle.com

As quickly as it can

It is only when we look at the screen

we realize this is not what we wanted!!

Where is Google?

You probably already know that it would be pointless shouting at the screen,

A waste of effort going in a mood,

you could threaten the computer and even cry!

But none of this will get you Google if you asked for Giggle

So we search the screen to see where we went wrong

And there it is ....

We see the 'I' where the 'o' should be

We delete the 'I' and replace with the 'o'

and hey presto!!!

UP comes Google

Exactly what we want

So we give it no more thought or consideration

It was just a typo -Nothing more nothing less

Just a typo and that can happen anytime to anyone….
And when it does,

There's no desktop or laptop available today
that can KNOW it's a typo

- and automatically correct it.

It can of course give you options as you type -

Auto typing or Auto fill

But it will not do anymore than offer possible suggestions
to what you may want -

BUT

You still have to be looking at the screen at the time
to see the auto fill option.

Computers are UNABLE pick up how we're feeling

They are UNABLE to 'read' our thoughts
or to know what we want

It can only ever know whatever information
we have installed on it beforehand.

To a computer keyboard there's no preference
to whether you are laughing,
or whether your are crying
as you program in the commands -

It will follow them exactly the same regardless.

5

HANDS FREE

HOW DO WE PROGRAMME OURSELVES WITHOUT A KEYBOARD?

Within your conscious mind there's no keyboard no mouse

And there's no monitor

So the way we program our neck top computers
Is done remotely

3 IS THE MAGIC NUMBER -

The magic number 3 plays an important role here
When Three internal senses out from five come into play
Then you have the equivalent to a mouse click

An instruction to 'run' that program -to start that feeling

The most common way I've come across for people to do this
is using Sight   (images in their minds eye)
Sound   (internal conversation about the image)
and Feelings

In any order

When You picture something in your minds eye
(negative or positive)

Then You say something to yourself about it
(negative or positive)

And so You feel a feeling inside yourself about or towards it
(negative or positive)

These three internal senses when used in unison
will create that specific program to run

Whether that's the result you want or not

Your neck top PC thinks you want it
And will do all it can to run this memory,
this behavior,   this response or feeling

Even if it is exactly the opposite to what the person wants
Hence why people are often getting results they do not want

Remember Google and giggle….
and just the same as the computer

Our neck top is unable to run anything apart from
that it was instructed to beforehand

6

INTENTION ALONE IS NOT ENOUGH

Often peoples successes in life
are determined by the programs they run in their mind

SOMETIMES THIS IS CALLED A WINNING MINDSET
IN SPORT OR BUSINESS

NOW - SCIENTISTS TELL US
THAT THE AVERAGE HUMAN MIND HAS
SOMEWHERE AROUND 40,000 THOUGHTS A DAY!

*Although they do say - 20,000 of those thoughts -
You had yesterday!

SO 20 THOUSAND NEW THOUGHTS PER DAY
20,000 thoughts!

That's impressive -
especially if you consider we probably think
we're not thinking about anything specific most of the time

Now obviously its impossible to MONITOR 20,000 thoughts

And of course when you have a thought -
you'll likely have a feeling with it

And its impossible to MONITOR 20,000 feelings

However - **It is possible** -

to MONITOR what it is **you say to yourself**
about those thoughts and feelings!

and it is THE WAY for success.

The words we use in our everyday language
has great meaning to us

And often as we know
one word can have many different meanings.

There are specific words in our language that we use everyday
And when we do we have a particular meaning in mind,
to our listener and to ourselves,

However more and more -
there's evidence to show the meaning of *certain specific* words

Is COMPETELY different to the one we intended

Our neck top pc has its own unique meaning for these words
And when used
specific responses within our mind can be noticed

PLEASE NOTE

<u>This is not a measure of your intention,</u>

<u>This is not a measure of your intelligence</u>

The same applies whether your 3 years old or 60 years old

Whether your never been to school or an Oxford Graduate

Our minds – our neck top computers
respond the same way to these certain words

Think about this

15 or 20 years ago
before home computers were common place

If you heard the word RAM
You would think of a male sheep -
that's the only meaning that word had

(unless of course this is your surname or your nickname)

Now we have computers everywhere

And even grandads are up to the minute
with their own USB sticks and IPods

So nowadays - if you hear the word RAM
Most people
would immediately think of something to do with computers

RAM - RANDOM ACCESS MEMORY

So RAM now has a very different meaning
since the birth of computers.

Google for some reason is very similar to our own neck top
response to certain words

For example

if you put in the word RAM into Google box

The search results you get will be predominantly related to
Random Access Memory

There may be ONE gratuitous result -
at the very bottom of the page

Almost like saying -
" could you mean a male sheep you crazy lady "

The specific words I'm going to share with you
are the main 'culprits' that I hear or read in everyday life
when I see people getting **exactly what it is they don't want.**

This may be anything -

From getting their toddler to eat their lunch
or not wet the bed.....
to getting our teenagers to tidy their room, respect us
and do well at school..

Then of course we have what it is *we* really want
within our jobs and our relationships,

not to mention what it is we want for ourselves.

We perhaps want to be a non smoker
We perhaps want to be slim and healthy
We perhaps want to drink less and laugh more
We want to let go of our issues and leave them in the past
We want our children to eat healthy
We want our boss to give us a pay rise
We want our partner to listen better
We want our teenagers to have respect for us

Yet mostly -especially in my line of work as a therapist

I meet people who

WANT www. Google.com

But are getting www. Giggle.com

They don't know how they're not getting the results they want

Because **they do really want them**

And may be spending a lot of time and effort
to achieve the results the desire

But still they struggle or Fail

Or perhaps they may have some degree of success for a time

And as they do this - as they struggle or fail -
they are more than likely to be beating themselves about it

Giving themselves a hard time

" I'm no good at this, I've not got the willpower or the _____ "

We make ourselves feel bad for not achieving success

Of course if the issue is something like smoking or overeating

Then often these internal 'hard times'

— lead to the very thing your trying to stay away from

So you feel = so bad you have a cigarette to relax.

Or

You feel so bad and useless anyway
you have packet of crisps
Or that bar of chocolate

Sound familiar?

Most people do no more
than give themselves more bad feelings -
If they fail at something they wanted to achieve

They never think to *look back*
and consider investigating where they may have went wrong.

Remember - the REALLY amazing thing is
when we use a computer
and we don't get the results on the page we want

We immediately take responsibility for this.

We instantly think " oh no what have I done?"

We scan the screen looking for OUR MISTAKE

And if someone else is using our computer -

We immediately hold them responsible and usually say
something like

" what have **you** done"

We never dream it could be the computer just fed
and bored running that program

Bored looking at your pictures -
or its tired

No - never considered

its our mistake

We went wrong somewhere

So we fix it -or we get someone who can to do it for us.

We would never consider shouting at the PC

Threatening to upgrade it

Making it feel bad

This would be ridiculous and pointless

We know and accept this.

Though most PC users will admit to actually giving this a go at some point only to realize it makes no difference!

Yet constantly we do it with ourselves,
our own neck top computers

Expecting that our bad mood, or our disappointment,
our sheer miserable feeling

Will *magically be enough* to get us the results we want

Its almost like we think
the worse we make ourselves feel about failure

The more likely we are to succeed tomorrow or next time.

Yet I'm confident
that if we listened in on successful people
and their internal dialogue

It will more likely be WAY more positive language

than someone who is struggling in the same situation.

7

THE POWER OF WORDS

I believe there is approximately 330+ influential words
we use to ourselves and others everyday

we deliver these words with our own ultimate meaning
and personal intention behind them of course.

And lets not forget the actual oxford dictionary of meaning too.
Which may or may not match ours.

However
if you actually pay attention while you read the words
and follow the instructions within them

Then you may be surprised to discover
what some of these words create
Within your minds eye

As I've said and its worth repeating

When we think things in our minds eye & create a picture
an emotion will automatically be evoked

And we will comment on this in some way to ourselves -
in our own internal voice.

This is what our neck top pc considers to be a double click

Or a 'RUN' command

There are some words that have the same outcome
within our neck top as others

So we can look closer at 5 of those words
at the same time

Don't, Can't, Shouldn't, Won't, Wouldn't

Whether these are used abbreviated like Don't
Or used fully as in do not

It makes no difference within or subconscious mind

The science behind this is

'The Subconscious Mind is unable to produce a Negative back into Reality'

So when we use negative commands such as DON'T

Our subconscious mind is unable to give us these back - in the way we meant

Its almost as if our subconscious mind has NO FILE for DON'T

** **neither does Google** **

So just like Google - when we use the word don't

We will get exactly what we don't want

For example

Lets say your getting a new bike - and you loath red ones
so you want anything but red

You go to the internet for some inspiration perhaps

Now
if you type into Google images
I don't want a red bike…..

Do you know what you'll get?

A very high percentage of red bikes
The very thing you wanted to avoid

You may get a few gratuitous blue or green bikes
But predominantly red bikes

Google is unable to comprehend
you actually wanted to avoid images of a red bike.

Your subconscious mind is even more 'narrow' -
in its search results, and whether you like it or not
Your mind, my mind
our minds are all the same

Our subconscious mind is unable to produce a negative
such as don't - back into reality

Follow my instructions that are next -

and you'll discover what is created as a result

You may need to follow all the examples listed
or perhaps

You'll realize it after the first one

Instruction 1 -

DON'T THINK OF BLUE TREE

Instruction 2 -

YOU CANT, WHATEVER YOU DO
IMAGINE THE QUEEN ON THE BACK OF A RHINO

Instruction 3 -

YOU SHOULDN'T, REALLY SHOULDN'T
CONSIDER SUCKING ON A LEMON
& HOW THAT WOULD TASTE

Instruction 4 -

YOU PROBABLY WONT WANT TO ,
SO REALLY YOU WONT
THINK OF TAKING ALL YOUR CLOTHES OFF
AND RUNNING UP & DOWN YOUR STREET NAKED!

Instruction 5 -

I WOULDN'T.... AND YOU WOULDN'T WANT TO

KEEP REPEATING THESE INSTRUCTIONS

OR MAKE UP YOUR OWN FOR FUN

UNTILL

<u>YOU NOTICE WHAT IS GOING ON INSIDE</u>

Now step by step here's what happens
As you read the words -
You Internally say them to yourself

i.e. don't think of a blue tree

Your subconscious mind responds like Google
As fast as it can give you results it will display them

HAVING NO FILE FOR DON'T SHOULDN'T
WOULDN'T OR CAN'T

Your subconscious mind misses it out

MISSES IT OUT COMPLETELY

Therefore the instruction your mind understands
and then follows is to
THINK OF A BLUE TREE

And so

In a nano-second
your subconscious mind gives you the image of a blue tree

BUT -

and this is applicable to even a 3yr old

You - your conscious mind -
understands the meaning behind the sentence

You -
Your conscious mind understands the instruction means

THINK OF *SOMETHING OTHER* THAN A BLUE TREE

So you consciously take the image away FAST

This often leads people to *miss the image in their conscious awareness*

And not be aware they thought it at all

<u>Infact</u>

In order to consciously decide
NOT to think about something
You really must Think About it First !!!!

So for the many smokers who are saying

" I **don't** want to pay £7 for a packet of cigarettes"
"I **shouldn't** be smoking so much"
"I **can't** let the kids see me smoking"
"I **hope** I don't get a cough like last year"

They actually imagine in their mind
the *very thing they don't want*

And their neck top thinks

They want that

And then they wonder why they find it so hard to stop easily.

Or

Those 'Slimmers' or 'Dieters'
who say things to themselves like

" I **don't** want to put on any more weight"

" I **can't** get any fatter"

" I **shouldn't** have any cake/crisps/chocolate"

Or
The sports player who speaks to themselves using words like

"I **don't** want to get beat again"

"We **can't** get any worse than last time"

"I **shouldn't** let defeat get to me"

Or
Parents think about the times you have said

" **Don't** just Eat the chips"

" You **cant** live on chips"

" You **can't** stay up with no sleep"

" **Don't** speak to me like that"

"**Don't** jump on the sofa"

" You **can't** leave your stuff lying there"

" You **shouldn't** expect your mum/dad to pick up after you"

"**Don't** go near the road"

Or
Those in relationships
experiencing 'difficult' times with their partners or friends,
and using statements like

"I **Don't** want to argue with you"

"I **Don't** want to carry on like this"

" You **shouldn't** treat me this way"

"You **can't** act/think/speak like that"

As you read the sentences previously -

You have likely noticed now,
the internal image created automatically
within the minds eye.

Its no real surprise

The parents using these language patterns
are likely struggling to influence their children in a positive way
and instead
their children may well seem to do all the things
the parents really don't want!

This is when it can seem almost as if -
the more you tell yourself, or someone else -
NOT to do, say or respond in a certain way

THE MORE THEY DO IT

This can make it too easy for some parents to conclude
its too difficult to get *their* children to eat new foods,
or do some chores.........

Thus leading to them give in and accept the behaviors

or

Maybe letting themselves get stressed out about it
each and every time the situation arises. ...
Resulting in everyone involved feeling 'bad'
towards that specific situation.....
Dreading it so much -

they may even avoid it all together!

<u>TRY</u>

Another word with a different meaning 'linguistically' than it does within our Neck top is the word "TRY"

This word is more often than not used IMMEDIATELY AFTER the word don't or shouldn't

Many people use this word when *stating their intention.*

For example

A smoker who wants to quit the habit may say something like

" I **don't** want to pay the money for cigarettes

I'm going to **TRY** to cut down from Monday"

Or

" I **don't** want to get a cough like last year"

"I'm going to **TRY** those patches/tablets"

The 'Slimmer' or 'Dieter' who says

" I **can't** put on any more weight"

"I'm going to **TRY** that new diet"

or

"I **don't** want these jeans to get any tighter"

"I'm going to **TRY** and start to exercise more"

The sports player/coach who tells themselves or others -

" I d**on't** want to get beat" -

" I'm going to **REALLY TRY** to win this time"

or

"We **can't** let them win" -

"Lets **TRY** to get ahead early"

or

"I **shouldn't** let nerves get to me/us"-

"I/We should **TRY** to stay relaxed"

The parent that declares

"**Don't** just eat the chips"

"**TRY** some of the vegetables"

or

" You **cant** leave your shoes/toys there" -

"**TRY** and tidy them away"

or

"You **shouldn't** make so much noise" -

"**TRY** to just calm down and behave"

The husband/wife/friend/partner who says

" I **don't** want to argue with you" -

"Lets **TRY** to stay calm and not raise our voices"

or

" You **shouldn't** speak to me that way" -

" **TRY** and treat me with some respect"

We actually already *know* within ourselves what the word Try really means

And we are using it to our advantage many times without even realizing it

Consider this

You go to the supermarket
You meet someone you know and after a short friendly chat perhaps saying statements such as

" We shouldn't let it go so long"
" Lets get together?"

So you both agree you would like to meet up

You end the conversation with
one person saying to the other something like

" I'll TRY and give you a ring and make arrangements"

Ultimately however
the phone call never takes place

And if you were to meet that person again another day
They are not in any way annoyed at your lack of phoning?!?

Why is this??

Because……..

Their subconscious mind
- just like yours

Notes AND RESPONDS to the following

" I'm going to **FAIL** to phone you"

"I'm going to *want* to phone you
and *I'm going to put effort into doing it*

But

I'm not going to *actually manage to do it*"

Or

Perhaps your going off on holiday from work for a few days
and you ask a colleague
if they can take care of some work stuff for you

and their reply is something like

" I'll **TRY** to do this for you"

Chances are
when you return from your break

<u>They will not have managed to do as you asked</u>

They will have tried of course

They maybe even put lots of effort and time into doing it -
and perhaps they might manage to get a little done on it

But ultimately failing to either complete it

IF they manage to do any at all!

Or

Consider a time

When you have invited someone to an event or celebration
when you ask them they reply saying something like

" I'll **try** to pop along for a bit"

"I'll **try** to get a babysitter/ night off"

In all likely hood your heart will have fell a little
when you heard this response

Something inside *you* knows they wont make it.

If I was to say
I was going to **TRY** to be at your house at 8pm

You would probably expect me a little later -

not at 8pm

Infact if I knocked your door at exactly 8pm
after saying I would **try**

You would likely be pretty surprised!!

So when you use the word TRY

**Your subconscious mind
effectively replaces that with Fail/Struggle**

So in turn
you are saying the following to your neck top pc -

" I **don't** want to smoke" -

"I **DO** want to smoke"
(image automatically created inside of smoking)

" I'm going to **TRY** to stop" -

"I'm going to **FAIL/STRUGGLE** to stop"
(corresponding image of failing created automatically inside)

" **Don't** just eat the chips" -

"**DO** just eat the chips"
(image inside created automatically for eating chips)

" **Try** and eat some vegetables" -

"**FAIL/STRUGGLE** to eat some of the vegetables"
(corresponding image of leaving the vegetables is created)

" I **don't** want to get heavier"-

"I **DO** want to get heavier"
(again corresponding image created for becoming heavier)

"I **don't** want to get beat" -

" I **DO** want to get beat"
(image created internally representing defeat)

"I **don't** want to argue with you" -

" I **DO** want to argue with you
(image created automatically inside representing arguing)

Just pay attention to the results you get
with yourself and others
When you use Don't, Can't, Shouldn't, Wouldn't and Try
in this way

When you use the words like Don't and Try
in situations you want success in

we are **accidentally** programming ourselves
(and others)

To make success a STRUGGLE at least

However if instead

we utilized these words

to create the very images we actually want

(described sometimes as 'reverse psychology')

Almost like **tricking our mind**
into *creating the internal images we want*
In order to run the responses and behaviors we really want.

This can be easier –
and Way more fun
than putting in the conscious mental effort required
to 'think positively'
or to take the time to create the internal images of ourselves
experiencing success.

Most people I have met find this positive thinking difficult,
and many are simply unable to imagine themselves
achieving success easily

For example

Pay attention to what image comes to mind
when you think of the following sentences
Instead of the previous ones

" I don't want to be a natural non smoker easily"

" I am going to TRY to make this hard"

" I don't want to just stop easily"

" I want to try and not succeed"

"I'm going to TRY to miss smoking"

"I'm going to TRY to notice other smokers"

" Don't eat the vegetables all up before the chips"

"Try to not eat every single vegetable"

" I don't expect you to enjoy the taste of _____ "

" You wont like the taste of this _____ "

"Don't pick up your shoes – try and leave them there"

"TRY and stay awake past (bedtime)o'clock"

"you don't have to remember everything you learn at school"

"I don't expect to achieve my target weight easily"

"I'm going to try really hard to miss my fattening foods"

"I don't want to really enjoy healthy foods"

"I can't imagine being my ideal size and shape"

"I don't expect to win the game easily"

"I can't imagine winning"

"I'm going to try and be nervous"

"I don't expect to feel confident"

"I can't expect you to understand my point of view"

"I don't imagine we can eliminate arguing completely"

"I'm going to try to stay annoyed"

"I don't want it to be perfect all the time"

Did you notice the internal images automatically created with the previous sentences?

More like the internal representations
that you do actually want?

Practice with these words and notice the results you get

LOSE

LOSING IS BAD   GAINING IS GOOD

Another word that has very negative affect
within our neck top PC

the word LOSE...

This word is influencing us from the moment we are conceived

It is accepted now by most that babies can hear in the womb
(once their neck-top PC is up and running)

So while they are listening to us in the outside world
picking up on our emotions
and to our responses - to our surroundings

we are already influencing them
and beginning to install the aversion to LOSING
that remains with us our entire lives.

This specific reaction within our neck top pc
to the word LOSE
is reinforced repeatedly throughout our childhood
in so many different ways

One of THE most common ways
we accidentally install this response to LOSING

is through Games

Think back to a time
when you taught someone younger than you
to play a certain game
Perhaps Draughts or Dominoes

Is it not true
that when you were showing them
how to actually play this game

**You have to make a REAL Conscious Effort
to automatically not just win**

You have to put thought into *not winning*

Our unconscious will *do its best* to play the winning shot
And you will have to *really be careful*
not to just win

Paying attention the whole time
so the other player - (the child)
can win

Then when we let them win the game

We encourage them to be delighted and celebrate !

We may even congratulate them

"Well done   you're the winner"

Then
you play the game again

And once more
You have to pay real attention not to win

Once again -
Perhaps because your learning them the game

and *you don't want them to lose heart*

You let them win again

And celebrate once again that they are the winner

"Well done you're the winner"

After a few games of you putting effort to **let them win**
You probably come to the point where you decide
you will let yourself win this game -

After all they cannot win everything.

<u>AND THAT SEEMS LIKE A GOOD LESSON -</u>

AND IT IS

<u>EXCEPT</u>

This time
when **You let yourself beat them**

And

They are the loser

Its unlikely you congratulate them

More likely you commiserate them

"Never mind let play again see if you win this time"

"Aaww bad luck - shall we see if you can beat me this time"

Or something similar

THERE IS ONLY ONE REASON FOR PLAYING AND THAT'S TO WIN

<u>LOSING IS BAD   - GAINING IS GOOD</u>

As I say to my clients when we are discussing this topic -

Even if we were to arrange a game of badminton

And while we traveled to play

I let you chant to yourself all the way there
(those people who have met me
will know how *impossible* for me that would be)

You chant all the way there -

"I want to lose this game"
"I want Pauline to win this game"

Or such like

I'm sure you will agree with me

**This would not prevent your feet
from moving at their normal speed
in reaction to the game.**

You would have to actually nail your feet to the floor
to ***stop them moving***

<u>**The same applies to losing anything**</u>

For example

Your handbag -
one you don't like maybe -

That ugly granny handbag your Auntie bought you last Xmas
and you would like nothing better than for it to fall apart
so you can stop using it!!

Even if you constantly told yourself
you wanted to lose your bag at the shopping center ....

That once again
would not cause that to happen

Infact quite the opposite would likely happen

You would be **more** *aware of your bag*
More aware of its presence with you

And therefore make it impossible to actually *lose it!!*

Consider the following..................

WHEN YOU PLAY CARDS -
DO YOU WANT TO WIN OR LOSE?

WHEN YOU PLAY BINGO -
DO YOU WANT TO WIN OR LOSE?

WHEN YOU ARGUE   -
DO YOU WANT TO WIN OR LOSE?

WHEN YOU ENTER A COMPETITION -
DO YOU WANT TO WIN OR LOSE?

DO YOU WANT TO LOSE YOUR SIGHT?

DO YOU WANT TO LOSE YOUR HEARING?

DO YOU WANT TO LOSE YOUR HOUSE?

DO YOU WANT TO LOSE YOUR JOB?

DO YOU WANT TO LOSE YOUR HAIR?

DO YOU WANT TO LOSE YOUR PARTNER?

DO YOU WANT TO LOSE YOUR REPUTATION?

DO YOU WANT TO LOSE YOUR CAR KEYS?

DO YOU WANT TO LOSE YOUR FRIENDS?

DO YOU WANT TO LOSE YOUR FAMILY?

DO YOU WANT TO LOSE YOUR BELONGINGS?

DO YOU WANT TO LOSE YOUR ……………

<u>THE LIST IS ENDLESS</u>

But I would guess
that ***no matter what was at risk of being lost*** -

It would be something ***you would rather not lose
Ideally***

You would perhaps rather
***choose to give it up,   give it away,
or throw it out?***

Even people who claim to *not be competitive*

Can't simply reverse something
Ingrained into their responses

Its not that our unconscious mind is competitive about the game

Its more that **we are Programmed to Gain
Not to lose** -

We have learned unconsciously that losing is bad

<u>**Losing is NEVER something anyone wants to do**</u>

UNLESS ITS WEIGHT

Weight is the *only thing* in peoples lives they want to lose

It's likely the only time they would use the word

And when we do -

When we use the word lose to ourselves

Its, *at the very least* **IGNORED**
by our Subconscious mind

It is **IGNORED**
because its unable to locate any appropriate files
to run a program/response associated with the word lose

Even if you manage to actually lose some weight
despite using the word lose –
Its highly likely
when your subconscious mind realizes
You've LOST something

- ANYTHING -

It will do its best to locate that.

Think about a time when you realize something is lost.......

most of us respond the same way -

We run through the options of where it may be
this seems to happen automatically

Even if the item is not something we desperately need.
Our subconscious mind
keeps thinking about where it may be
Until its found.

Weight issues - *in my opinion*
begin **long before**
the first recognition of excess flab/ wobbly bits…..
and certainly long before any talk of diets

Where it all begins

From the first appointment to confirm the pregnancy,
the ritual of keeping track of mums weight begins

Discussions take place between friends, doctors, midwifes and relatives.

Asking how much weight mum has put on so far
What weight her 1st baby was *-if applicable*
What weight she and dad were

Over and over this conversation will be repeated

**ALL THE TIME
BABY IS LISTENING IN**

Then the happy day comes
When the baby arrives
Everyone has the same 2 questions -

"IS IT A GIRL OR A BOY?"

"WHAT DO THEY WEIGH ?"

This latter is more often than not
followed up with either a sympathetic or *comforting comment*

Or a squeal of delight/surprise and *congratulations on the size*

This continues and gathers momentum as it goes

ALL THE TIME
BABY IS LISTENING & LEARNING

The weight of baby
and ***their food intake*** and output
is *Greatly discussed and monitored* in the hospital
by the doctors and nurses

And then *again by mums and visitors*

So by the time mum and baby get home
and the home visitors begin to arrive -
even first time mums are quite familiar with the procedure

It's the same ritual that's done with every baby I've ever known

Each and every well meaning visitor that arrives now
and for the next few months at the very least

The health visitors, the grannies, the aunts, the neighbours
All want to know the same information
how are the **feeding**? & what's their **weight** now?

ALL THE TIME BABY IS LISTENING IN

Mum will normally reply
with either an update on how *well the little one is eating*
and/or
how much weight they have put on in the last week or so

"Oh he's great - taking 4 ounces per feed now!!
And he is up to 11lb!"

This will be met with great delight
And maybe even an affectionate comment such as

"wee pudding"
Or
"chubby wee cheeks"

**Along with happy smiles
and positive energy filling the room.**

Of course
mum will rarely be so full of happy smiles and delight
if baby has **lost** some weight that week

If they have **not eaten so well**
and have perhaps dropped their intake per feed

"Oh not so good" with an accompanying *concerned tone*

"He's only taking 3 oz in a bottle
and he lost half a lb this week -
that's him down to 8lb now"

He should be nearer to 9lb
(*should be* is often according to what he eat/put on last week

or

something that has been said to the mum by another mum

or

according to what a previous sibling took at that age.

The reaction to this news about weight loss
is concern and worry -
Possibly followed with suggestions to improve this

"Have you tried that new formula...?"

"Have you tried bathing him before a feed
see if he *eats More?*"

"Maybe there is something wrong
and you should take him to the doctor"

All manner of advice and ideas will be given
to ***avoid baby having to lose any more weight*****.....**

ALL THE TIME BABY IS LISTENING & LEARNING

Baby is getting the feeling
losing weight is not good already

Even if they don't understand why
they are aware of the reaction and attention it is creating

consider this...........

How many times have you,
or someone you know been feeding a baby
and when the little one *refuses* the last half ounce of the formula

we or they,
do all we can do get them to *finish the bottle*?

Then we/ they feel so proud of themselves
if they do manage it

*"C'mon you've only got a mouthful left -
and your going to finish it"* -

sound familiar?

*Of course this is all done with love and the babies best
interests at heart*

But nonetheless

We are already programming our little ones neck top PC

**Beginning the installation of the beliefs & responses
we want back from them as they grow.**

Now

Because our clever little cherub is *communicating to us*
Doing their best to tell us *they are full*
Or they have *had enough*

Maybe they feel a little bloated
Or they just don't quite have the appetite *right now*

But basically
baby is in the early days of
learning how to respond to their own feelings.

Learning how to Respond
to their own internal levels and limits

They let us know perhaps by losing interest in the bottle
and turning their heads away

"No more mum" - baby says

Holding up the bottle
We look at what's left in the feed

Even if we conclude
there is maybe only a mouthful or two   in the bottom…

What we are effectively saying
with our actions that follow -

**"No your not full,
I'll tell you when your full"**

"IGNORE your instincts and listen to mine!!!"

Then we then do our best to get baby to take whats left

Maybe we will *wriggle* and *push the bottle back in*
Using encouraging words to the *already stuffed baby*

Doing *all we can* to get them to take the last two mouthfuls

We feel elated if baby takes it for us
And other people may even congratulate us on this talent

"Well done you -
getting him to finish it"

"You feed him -
you can get him to finish his bottle"

**The individual personality of the baby
will have some influence here to how baby responds
when exposed to these surroundings and influences***

Read my coming book on
BABYS PERSONALITIES IN PREGNANCY AND
INFANCY.

But suffice to say whatever their reaction

whether they actually finish the bottle or not

We will have given them the clear message
to **keep eating**....

to eat beyond this feeling they have now...

To ignore their internal signals and listen to us

Babies learn from us

We all *know and accept this*
Yet do we ever

STOP to consider WHAT we are REALLY communicating
in these type circumstances?

**"IGNORE YOUR INSTINCTS AND LOOK OUTSIDE YOURSELF
TO KNOW IF YOUR FULL YET"**

Now on the other hand
if the baby is what is perceived to be a *Good Eater* -

One of those little ones
that always finishes what gets offered to them
Infact may even perhaps be *looking for more…*

Perhaps you have known children who
reliably finish their portion straight off -
no hesitation….no fuss

**And most of the parents with these children
I have experienced**

Do what when their little one polishes their meal off ?

INCREDIBLY

They think baby might **still** feel a bit hungry!!!
And we wouldn't want that guilt- (separate issues)

So they attempt to give them more food!!!
MORE FOOD!!

I have witnessed with my own eyes
lots of parents who wont actually stop feeding a child

Until the child is protesting
is sick
or falls asleep!!

So inevitably
the same message is being replayed in the babies mind

<u>Keep eating</u> -
Ignore this feeling of being full

Just keep eating   ignore your own internal signals!

Our well meaning relatives, babysitters and visitors
react to these *little 'lunch buckets'*
in a **very Positive way**

Often *Congratulating mum*
on having a baby with such a healthy appetite saying

"That's such a good thing he's eating so well"

"He'll grow to be a big strong boy -
just like his Dad/Grandad/Uncle...."

REMEMBER

BABY IS LISTENING ALL THE TIME

And by now,
baby will be starting to get the message that

**People seem to react NEGATIVELY around them
when they are 'losing'**

They may not understand why

But It doesn't go down well   seems people don't like it

And it does create a lot of fuss and attention around baby
The general atmosphere of concern and worry
may surround these babies

Whereas the good eater will be getting lots of attention
in an *encouraging way* -

Lots of smiles and old people pinching their *chubby wee cheeks*

"What a wee pudding - He's adorable"

ONCE AGAIN THE BABIES PERSONALITY
COMES INTO PLAY
AS TO HOW THEY WILL REACT TO THIS

LOSING IS BAD -
The reaction of everyone when babies weight goes down

GAINING IS GOOD -
The reaction of everyone when babies weight increases

This communication continues
and as the child develops
and becomes more complex and individual -
so does the message given to them

By the time the child is a toddler
and begin feeding themselves,
and they are being introduced to new textures and tastes...

Often we parents
are already *subconsciously expecting problems*

We are *led to believe* by tv programmes and the media
that *'children don't like veg or healthy foods'*

They want sweets and snacks
And todays parents
will have to find positive ways to introduce new foods -
and they may struggle to get the healthy stuff down there necks.

Because
we want our children to grow up healthy and strong -

This sadly can lead to parents serving portions way too big.

Even though
they're already half expecting they wont actually finish it all -

Some parents will still
pile it on that plate

Especially if the child has mentioned being hungry
or informs us they love fish fingers !!!!

The parents seem to think
if they just put it on the plate then

MAYBE - JUST MAYBE

They wont notice and they take the chance

The child *just might eat a little more than they would normally..*

Another effect of this influence can be

what I call *Training 4 Failure* -

where

**<u>we are accidentally
putting our children in a position to fail</u>**

As opposed to

SETTING OUR KIDS UP FOR SUCCESS -

Setting things up so our *children are unable to fail easily* -

This then
**gets them used to the feelings of Success
and Feeling Proud.**

When the parent decides to take the opportunity
to *put a little more* carrots on the plate
or add *an extra fish finger*

There will,
at some point be the inevitable conversation
between the parent and child
debating whether or not they have eaten enough
and are indeed full.

<u>Consider the following -</u>

FULL
is something we unfortunately *cannot see with our eyes*
Nor can we *hear any signs of being full*

FULL
is only something <u>we can only feel</u>
And *only the person actually experiencing it* can feel it

No one can feel full or hungry for another person!

Yet we continue along this path
slowly programming & brainwashing our children
to look for approval - *somewhere else outside themselves*
to know if they have eaten enough

We *bribe them/ coax them/ punish them*
to get them to eat

what **WE** consider to be
a sufficient amount in a day…

Using statements such as

"Your not finished until you eat 3 more carrots"

"Your Gran/Aunt cooked that lovely meal
the least you can do is finish it" - GUILT

"You wont grow" - POOR SELF IMAGE

"You will get no pudding" - PUNISHMENT

"There's so many children in this world
who would be glad of that food" GUILT

"If you eat it all/ a bit more
you can have an ice cream" REWARD

"You will go to bed early" - CONFINEMENT/SOLITUDE

"You'll get it again for supper/breakfast" - PUNISHMENT

All of these were said to me as a child
And I heard parents all throughout my life say the same

I have even said some of these myself
Before I knew otherwise of course!!!

On the other hand the children with the healthy appetite-
They are the ones who will hear comments such like

"Oh that's the stuff -
Your going to grow up to be big and strong"

"Well done - you can come to my house for tea anytime"

"What a compliment to the chef"

"As a treat for eating all your dinner -
you can have the biggest piece of cake/pudding"

"That's what I like to see - a nice clean plate"

All of these were said to my best friend growing up
as she was a good eater as opposed to me being a poor eater

The whole time this is happening the program of

LOSING IS BAD GAINING IS GOOD

is being reinforced over and over
until this becomes a hidden habit –
an automatic response we are not even aware of

8

PROGRAMMING OTHERS

When we are communicating with each other
We are as good as controlling the programs their neck top 'runs'

We are aware that 'mind control' exists
But perhaps do not realize
that this is something we are ALL capable of doing

And infact

We are ALL actually doing this constantly
throughout our interactions with others

Whether we mean to or not!

Infact from the moment
we start giving instructions our to our children
we are beginning the installation of programs/responses

Statements like……

"DON'T TOUCH THAT"
are often the first things we say

Of course this is done with love
and from the heart

But nonetheless

our childrens neck tops respond
in the very same way as ours does

So their neck top **hears**
and **gives internal images to match** -

DO TOUCH THAT!!

And then of course

Their neck top then thinks
they want to run the program to 'touch'

Then we wonder
why they keep going back to touch the same thing
repeatedly!!

We are accidentally triggering
often unwanted or unproductive programs in others around us.

Another example is when we say to our friend or partner

" I DONT WANT TO ARGUE WITH YOU"

"TRY TO UNDERSTAND MY POINT OF VIEW"

"DON'T SPEAK TO ME LIKE THAT"

" I DON'T MEAN TO HURT YOU"

"YOU SHOULDN'T TREAT ME LIKE THIS"

"I DON'T WANT TO GO ON LIKE THIS"

More often than not
these statements only fuel any animosity
and bad feeling already present.
Simply because they create the internal images that are
effectively the very opposite to what the speakers intends.

Similarly the coach or trainer who says to the team -

"WE DON'T WANT TO GET BEAT"

"WE CAN'T AFFORD TO LOSE ANYMORE POINTS"

"WE NEED TO TRY TO WIN THIS GAME/MATCH"

"WE SHOULDN'T LET THEM GET AHEAD"

9

THE KEY TO PROGRAMMING OTHERS

**Assuming this information is being read
and applied by
those with only Good intentions***

Because like everything else in life

This could be misused
by those who want to negatively influence others.

Infact after reading this information

you may begin to actually notice certain eye opening things

in your everyday life.....

How

those around you
have perhaps occasionally been programming YOU

It may only be to get a cup of coffee

Or some other harmless gain

But perhaps
you've already thought of the way they are doing this?

Are they using the don't or shouldn't?

Or perhaps its Try they utilize to their own benefit.......

Or Maybe,

You are now beginning to understand

how **you** have either deliberately or accidentally
programmed others

In a positive or negative way.

Lets assume you want to learn
how to get the best out of your children

Three (3) once again is the magic number

We must ensure
we put the 'program' we want in three (3) times

Of course this will be very suspicious
if we just repeat the same words 3 times

Even a four year old will probably notice if we did that!

So to combat this

We must bypass the conscious mind -

'The Operator'

Because one of the main 'jobs' of our conscious mind

Is to act as our *'critical filter'* to the outside world

Protecting us from just accepting everything we hear or see

Its our conscious minds role
to question what we see and hear outside ourselves

It is infact our conscious mind
that would be the part of our mind to react
to something we consider to be

Untrue,

Unacceptable,

Unbelievable

Unachievable

or Unrealistic

So in order to bypass this 'critical filter'

We need to say the words 3 times

IN A DIFFERENT WAY EACH TIME

Yet still worded in a way
that ensures their neck top pc
Creates the internal images you require
for them to run the program you want

This is something that, with a little practice
can be a great positive benefit to yourself and others

Take this example -

Fill 2 glasses with water
ALL THE WAY TO THE TOP

Ask someone to
" put them over there on the table/worktop"
Then follow this with

"AND DON'T SPILL THE WATER ON MY CARPET"

As they are halfway across say -
"TRY NOT TO SPILL THAT WATER NOW"

And just before they reach the table/worktop
"REALLY YOU SHOULDN'T SPILL ANY
OF THAT WATER ON MY CARPET"

As you do this WATCH THEIR FACE not the glasses
And you will notice the signs of an internal 'dilemma'

Their neck to PC is hearing
and responding to -

" SPILL THE WATER ON MY CARPET"

" FAIL NOT TO SPILL THAT WATER NOW"

"REALLY **YOU SHOULD SPILL THAT WATER**
ON MY CARPET"

The images created internally will match the above commands
And in turn the neck top will treat this as a 'click'

The instruction to 'run' this program

Remember

Our neck top is UNABLE to reason or debate with us

Our neck top is designed to **FOLLOW INSTRUCTION**

Even though the person carrying the glasses understands
the meaning behind our words

They know we mean

" KEEP ALL THE WATER IN THE GLASS"

&

"MAKE SURE MY CARPET STAYS DRY"

THIS is what creates the internal dilemma
between following the instructions given

-TO SPILL THE WATER

And doing their best to

-KEEP THE WATER IN THE GLASS

Our neck top will do as it is designed to do -

FOLLOW INSTRUCTIONS

And will do its utmost to SPILL THE WATER

And will therefore cause something inside -

Like a sneeze , hiccup
or maybe even causing them to trip up over their own feet!!

Resulting in a little of the water spilling!!!

Now
Our neck top pc can move on to the next instruction.

10

THE MAGIC NUMBER 3

Throughout history
the number 3 has been considered by many as a magic number

In some interpretations of numerology
the number 3 is seen as a symbol of completeness

And the number 3 is seen by many as a lucky number

Mathematics refer to the number 3
as the first LUCKY PRIME NUMBER

And for the science lovers -

the symbolic importance of the 3 follows

Consider this

Atoms -the basic buildings blocks of life
consist of 3 constituents
PROTONS NEUTRONS & ELECTRONS

Matter has 3 basic States -
LIQUID SOLID & GAS

The Earth itself is made up of 3 main layers
CORE MANTLE & THE CRUST

Light is comprised of the 3 primary colours
RED BLUE & GREEN

The Atmosphere is made with the 3 main molecules
OXYGEN CARBON & HYDROGEN

We humans are made up of the same 3 molecules
OXYGEN CARBON & HYDROGEN

We humans process 3 main substances for energy
FATS CARBOHYDRATES & PROTEINS

We humans perceive everything in 3 dimensions

We humans have 3 trimesters of pregnancy

We humans have 3 basic reactions states -
FLIGHT FREEZE & FIGHT

There are 3 main archetypal influences
WARRIOR SETTLER & NOMAD

consider how many times
the number 3 plays a significant part in our world

And in our everyday lives, our language etc

In religions from all over the world
they worship a divine trinity

i.e. The father the son & the holy spirit

We have a PAST PRESENT FUTURE

We have a TOP MIDDLE & BOTTOM

We start a race with
READY STEADY GO

We launch rockets with 3 2 1

Dorothy (wizard of oz) had to
TAP HER HEELS TOGETHER 3 TIMES

We have THE GOOD THE BAD & THE UGLY

Our class system-
LOWER MIDDLE & UPPER

We are recommended to have 3 MEALS A DAY

We reward 3 places in a competition -
GOLD SILVER & BRONZE

Books and Stories have a
START A MIDDLE & AN END

We have
YESTERDAY TODAY & TOMORROW

We have 3 stages of LABOUR (childbirth)

We eat 3 course meals with
STARTER MAIN COURSE & PUDDING

We have 3 stages of learning
BEGINNER, INTERMEDIATE & EXPERT

We say to each other

IT COMES IN THREES

ITS AS SIMPLE AS A B C

HIP HIP HOORAY

WE HAVE 3 WISHES ON OUR BIRTHDAY CAKE

These are just a few that come mind -

I'm sure you can think of many more yourself

It seems
whether you are scientifically/logically orientated
or lean to the spiritual, mystical and esoteric

The number '3' will likely mean something important to you
within your psyche.

11

SYMBOLISM

By now you may be realizing
Our mind thinks in pictures –
The zip files I mentioned in chapter 3

The images we hold in our minds eye,
are the equivalent to
the 'programs' we're instructing our neck top *to run tomorrow.*

These images – Good or bad

Are creating our future reality.

In my experience

Lots of people find it *hard to consciously create positive images* and many find it much more automatic for them to imagine what they *don't want*

Or they *forget to 'think positively'*
and before they know it they find themselves
stuck in a rut of negative internal images and feelings.....

They lose sight of their Goal.........

One Simple way to work through this
and to **remind yourself of your Goal**
is to use Symbolism

(just like using the zip file icon image)

The power of Symbolism on our responses
has been known by many cultures and individuals
and been utilized by many
for thousands of years

This has had many different names
including the more modern you may recognise

Cosmic Ordering
The Law of Attraction
The Science of getting rich
The Law of Abundance

A recent enthusiast of cosmic ordering (Symbolism)
is our very own Mr Noel Edmonds,
he's openly talked of his belief in this ancient 'Influence Ritual'

On his 'Deal or No Deal' tv show,
he can clearly be seen using Symbolism (little images)
on his hand.

He has been interviewed and quoted many times about this.

He credits the tv show contract to cosmic ordering
and his consultations with Barbel Mohr
(consultant and author on Cosmic Ordering)

What is Symbolism and Cosmic Ordering?

Put Simply

it is

What You *Think and Feel* About

You *Bring About*

So it really pays to

Think about Your Goal – Your Intention in life

If you want to be a non smoker - then think about being a HAPPY HEALTHY CONFIDENT non smoker FEELING THE WAY YOU WANT TO FEEL

Think about this – A LOT!

If you want to be thinner - then again think about being a HAPPY, CONFIDENT, HEALTHY, SLIM person WEARING THE CLOTHES AND FEELING THE WAY YOU WANT TO FEEL

Think about this – A LOT!

This is what the images on Noels hand were about.

The Simple Steps to make it easier to

REMIND YOURSELF
TO THINK ABOUT YOUR GOAL........

A LOT!

STEP ONE -

Take the time to think about your goal

Think about achieving your goal

THINK ABOUT SUCCESS

<u>AS IF YOU ALREADY HAVE IT</u>

REALLY THINK ABOUT IT

ACCESS WHAT SUCCESS WILL LOOK LIKE

ACCESS WHAT SUCCESS WILL FEEL LIKE

ACCESS WHAT SUCCESS SOUNDS LIKE

EVEN ACCESS THE SMELL OF SUCCESS

Really take the time to complete Step 1 to achieve best results

STEP TWO -

Think of the simplest image that to you,
Represents SUCCESS IN YOUR GOAL

Perhaps this may be a particular shape – like a heart or a smiley face, a bright sunshine or maybe a £ sign.

Any simple image that immediately makes you think of

SUCCESS IN YOUR GOAL

STEP THREE -

Now draw your image everywhere!

Anywhere you will see it – and automatically
Think about Success.

Draw it On your diary, Your telephone pad,

Your kitchen wipe clean board........

Or

Like Noel you might choose to draw it on your hand.

So every time you use your hand

Again you are Reminded
of how Success Looks, Feels, Sounds and Smells

this then of course

RUNS THE PROGRAM OF SUCCESS
WITHIN YOUR NECK TOP.

I hope you enjoyed reading

Please take the time to leave a review on Amazon
or some feedback via email – info@Success4Self.co.uk

Look out for my next book with more information
on the other everyday words we use
and there true meaning ……..
including

BECAUSE, BUT, WONDER, WHY and HOW

"Sleep is unconscious meditation

Meditation is conscious sleep" -*Deepak Chopra*

Printed in Great Britain
by Amazon